A
DIFFERENT
WORLD

DYSLEXIA

BY
ROBIN TWIDDY

KidHaven
PUBLISHING

Published in 2022 by
KidHaven Publishing, an Imprint of Greenhaven Publishing, LLC
353 3rd Avenue
Suite 255
New York, NY 10010

Edited by: John Wood
Designed by: Gareth Liddington

Cataloging-in-Publication Data

Names: Twiddy, Robin.
Title: Dyslexia / Robin Twiddy.
Description: New York : KidHaven Publishing, 2022. | Series: A different world | Includes glossary and index.
Identifiers: ISBN 9781534538443 (pbk.) | ISBN 9781534538467 (library bound) | ISBN 9781534538450 (6 pack) | ISBN 9781534538474 (ebook)
Subjects: LCSH: Dyslexia--Juvenile literature. | Dyslexic children--Juvenile literature.
Classification: LCC RJ496.A5 T95 2022 | DDC 618.92'8553--dc23

Printed in the United States of America

CPSIA compliance information: Batch #CSKH22: For further information contact Greenhaven Publishing LLC, New York, New York at 1-844-317-7404.

Please visit our website, www.greenhavenpublishing.com. For a free color catalog of all our high-quality books, call toll free 1-844-317-7404 or fax 1-844-317-7405.

This book was written and designed with accessibility for people with color vision deficiency and dyslexia in mind.

Photo credits:

Cover & Throughout – CkyBe, Serhii Bobyk, Evgenii Emelianov, KerrysWorld, kryzhov, Pixel-Shot, 2&3 – VanoVasaio, 4&5 – Monkey Business Images, wavebreakmedia, 6&7 – Sergey Nivens, Roman Samborskyi, 8&9 – bysora, Khosro, Decha Laoharuengrongkun, Darya Palchikova, ankudi, 10&11 – David Franklin, 12&13 – Photographee.eu, Stock-Asso, 14&15 – Kuttelvaserova Stuchelova, wavebreakmedia, 16&17 – Madhourse, myboys.me, xavier gallego morell, 18&19 – GOLFX, wavebreakmedia, 20&21 – GagliardiPhotography, Ruslan Huzau, 22&23 – Sergey Mikheev, spass.

All facts, statistics, web addresses, and URLs in this book were verified as valid and accurate at time of writing.
No responsibility for any changes to external websites or references can be accepted by either the author or publisher.

CONTENTS

Words that look like <u>this</u> can be found in the glossary on page 24.

A DIFFERENT WORLD?

We all live in the same world, don't we? Well, for some people who have a <u>condition</u> known as dyslexia, the world can look a little different.

In this book you will have the chance to see what the world looks like for someone with dyslexia. It is important to understand how others see the world and the challenges they face.

WHAT IS DYSLEXIA?

Most people need to learn language that is both spoken and written. This helps us talk to each other. People who have dyslexia have a bit more trouble with language than others.

Our brains store lots of information about words. We need to learn how words are written, how they are <u>pronounced</u>, and the rules that make them work together in a sentence.

A person with dyslexia has more trouble storing these rules and making sense of them.

BUT WHAT DOES IT MEAN?

Dyslexia isn't the same for everyone who has it. Here are some of the things that a person with dyslexia might experience:

Reading some words wrong

Trouble saying some words

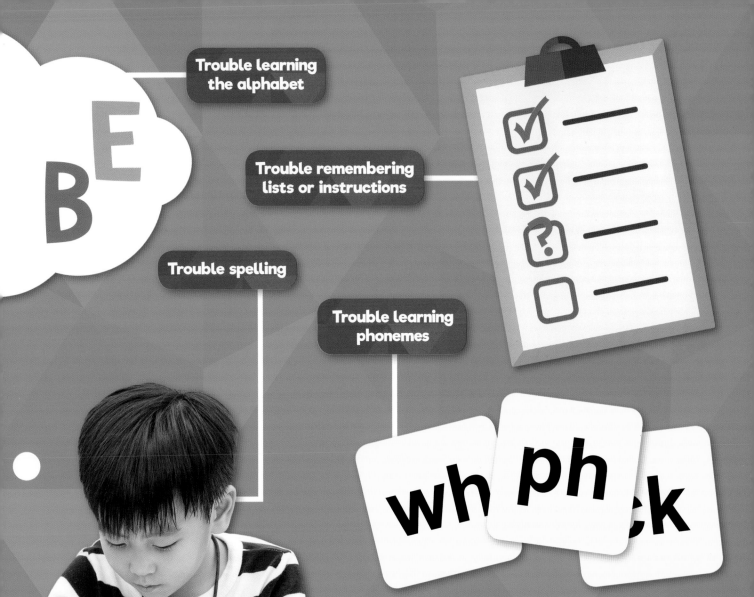

Trouble learning the alphabet

Trouble remembering lists or instructions

Trouble spelling

Trouble learning phonemes

These are just some of the things that a person with dyslexia might have to face. They might experience all of these, or just a few. Everyone is different.

9

READING INSTRUCTIONS

HOMEWORK

TASK: Your family is being visited by the Barkman family. The Barkman family enjoys food made by children.

You will need an adult to help you with this homework.

NOW:
1: Make them a sandwich with an adult.
2: Make them a cup of tea or coffee with an adult.

NOW:
A. Write out the instructions for making a sandwich.

B. Write out the instructions for making a cup of tea for the Barkmans.

The whole class has been given instructions for their homework. Karla's friends don't have much trouble reading and following the instructions.

However, Karla has dyslexia and she finds it a bit more difficult to read these instructions.

Date   No.

HOMEWORK

TASK: Your family is being visited by the Barkman family. The Barkman family enjoys food made by children.

You will need an abult to help you with thishomework.

NOW:
1: Make them asandwich with an abult.
2: Make them a cup of tae or coffee with an adult.

WON:

A. Write out the instructions for making a sandwich.

B. Write out the instructions for making a cup of tea for the Barkmans.

This isn't what Karla sees, but it shows us how the words can get jumbled in her mind.

Even though the instructions are the same, Karla's dyslexia makes it hard for her to tell some letters apart or to make sense of some of the spaces.

Other Ways to Share Information

Written instructions are not always the best way to tell people with dyslexia what to do. Instructions might make more sense by using pictures and <u>diagrams</u>.

Using <u>audio</u> recordings or video recordings can be a better way of sharing information with a person with dyslexia. It just depends on the person.

Some people with dyslexia find it much easier to make sense of information when they hear it.

A DIFFERENT WAY OF THINKING

Even though people with dyslexia can find reading and writing more difficult, this does not mean that they are not smart. People with dyslexia can be really good at thinking in different ways.

Some of the skills that people with dyslexia are often stronger in are:

- **Thinking about 3D shapes**
- **Spotting patterns and things that don't fit**
- **Creative activities such as painting, drawing, and acting**

People with dyslexia are often really good "out of the box" thinkers. That means they think about problems in new and different ways.

15

DYSLEXIC SUCCESS

Some famous writers have had dyslexia.

There are a lot of very successful people with dyslexia, such as <u>entrepreneurs</u>, actors, painters, filmmakers, and <u>astrophysicists</u>.

Even though dyslexia can make it difficult to do schoolwork, many people with dyslexia have proven that they are just as smart as anyone else. They just think about problems in different ways.

There have been U.S. presidents with dyslexia.

IT'S NOT JUST READING

When people think about dyslexia, they usually think about problems with reading and writing. But a person with dyslexia can have other problems with language.

Some people who have dyslexia might have trouble remembering a word or how to pronounce it. This doesn't mean that they don't understand the word. It just means that their brains aren't as quick at finding that information.

SUPPORT

There is a lot of support for people who are struggling with schoolwork because of their dyslexia. The type of support depends on what difficulties their dyslexia creates.

Some people with dyslexia may find that different-colored paper helps them order words on the page better. Sometimes they just need a little longer to do a task. Extra one-on-one classes with the teacher might also help some students.

This boy is listening to an **audiobook** instead of reading off the page.

WE ARE ALL DIFFERENT

People with dyslexia work hard because of the challenges they face.

Having dyslexia can make many things challenging, such as following instructions, reading signs quickly, or remembering lists of things.

Even though people who have dyslexia like Karla may see the world a little differently, we are more alike, all of us, than we are different.

GLOSSARY

3D shapes   shapes with height, width, and depth
astrophysicists   people who study space and the stars
audio   having to do with sound
audiobook   a recording of a book being read aloud
condition   an illness or other medical problem
diagrams   pictures that show how something works or is done
entrepreneurs   people who start and run a business
pronounced   how something is said

INDEX